PRACTICE
THE
PRESENCE OF GOD

BY BROTHER LAWRENCE

New Revised Version in Modern English

D0167896

PRACTICE
THE
PRESENCE OF GOD

BY BROTHER LAWRENCE

New Revised Version in Modern English

REVISED BY
JIM JOHNSON

RESET PUBLISHING

Practice the Presence of God by Brother Lawrence
New Revised Version in Modern English
Copyright © 2009 by James C. Johnson II (aka Jim Johnson)
Reset Publishing an Imprint of JC Publishing House - San Jose, CA.

ISBN-10: 0-9815905-4-3
ISBN-13: 978-0-9815905-4-7

Original Material is Public Domain:
The Practice of the Presence of God: The Best Rule of Holy Life
Conversations and Letters of Brother Lawrence (Nicholas Herman),
c. 1605-1691 first published sometime after 1691 by Joseph de Beaufort
Electronic Public Domain Version: BLPPOG10.xxx-1.0

All Rights Reserved Worldwide. No portion of this book may be reproduced, stored in a retrieval system or transmitted in any form or by any means – electronic, mechanical, photocopy, recording, scanning or other - except for brief quotations in critical reviews or articles, without the prior written permission of the author or publisher.

Disclaimer: The author has made his best effort to maintain the integrity of the original intent of the material while revising it from Old English to Modern English. The theological ideas presented in this book are solely the ideas of Brother Lawrence and not necessarily the author of this book (Practice the Presence of God: New Revised Version in Modern English).

All Scripture quotations are taken from the New King James Version®. Copyright © 1982 by Thomas Nelson, Inc. Used by permission. All rights reserved.

Printed in the USA

Note to all Readers

This
New Revised Version in Modern English

Practice the Presence of God

By Jim Johnson

TO ALLOW THE READER THE ABILITY TO EASILY
WRITE SMALL NOTES OR COMMENTS
IN THE BOOK

WE HAVE DESIGNED THIS BOOK WITH
WIDER OUTSIDE MARGINS

Table of Contents

★

Chapter   **Page**

Forward by Jim Johnson   13

Brother Lawrence – A brief history   17

First Conversation - Bro. Lawrence speaks with Joseph   21
de Beaufort about his conversion and his work at the
Monastery. He also shares his thoughts on faith,
surrender and satisfaction in God's presence.

Second Conversation - Bro. Lawrence shares with   25
Joseph de Beaufort on a variety of topics including the
need for love to be the motive driving everything we do.

Third Conversation - Bro. Lawrence discusses with   31
Joseph de Beaufort his thoughts about: faith working by
love; that natural work is no hindrance to sensing God's
presence; and the need for complete surrender.

Fourth Conversation – Bro. Lawrence discussed with   35
Joseph de Beaufort with great openness of heart
concerning his approach to God.

First Letter - Bro. Lawrence describes how the habitual   43
sense of God's Presence was found.

Chapter	Page

Second Letter - Bro. Lawrence writes about the difference between himself and others. He consistently and persistently pursues faith alone. He disputes the charge of being delusional. — 47

Third Letter - Bro. Lawrence writes about a soldier friend whom he encourages to trust in God. — 55

Fourth Letter - Bro. Lawrence writes of himself in the third person, and encourages his correspondent to press on to fuller practicing of the Presence of God. — 57

Fifth Letter - Bro. Lawrence prays for a sister who is about to make a commitment to Christian service and shares about a fresh insisting upon the necessity and virtue of practicing the Presence of God. — 61

Sixth Letter - Written to a member of the Monastery who had received from him a book and to whom he again expounds on his favorite topic: encouragement to persevere. — 65

Seventh Letter - At the age of nearly eighty, Bro. Lawrence writes to a man who is sixty-four, to live and die with God and promises and asks for prayer. — 69

Eighth Letter - Bro. Lawrence writes about wandering thoughts that occur during times of prayer. — 71

Ninth Letter - A letter to a corresponding sister, whom he regards with respect tinged with fear. He shares again concisely his reoccurring theme. — 73

Chapter	Page

Tenth Letter - Bro. Lawrence has difficulty, but sacrifices his will, to write as requested to a person who has lost a friend and shares that his loss may lead to an acquaintance with The Friend.   77

Eleventh Letter - Bro. Lawrence is writing to someone who is in great pain and tells him God is the Physician of body and of soul and that he would gladly suffer at God's wish.   79

Twelfth Letter - Probably written to the same person. He expresses his own lasting comfort through faith.   83

Thirteenth Letter - To the same person he exhorts him to have a fuller and complete confidence in God, for his body and soul.   85

Fourteenth Letter - Bro. Lawrence expresses gratitude for the mercies and the amount of relief the recipient of this letter has experienced, while he has himself been near death, nevertheless he too has been comforted during his suffering.   87

Fifteenth Letter - Brother Lawrence wrote this letter soon before his death in 1691.   89

About the Author and his Wife   93

Missionary and Berlin Ministry Information   95

Books and Media by Jim Johnson   97

Forward

★

James 4:14
*For what is your life? It is even a vapor that appears
for a little time and then vanishes away.*

Life is short! We must choose how we will spend the few years God has granted us on this earth. Will they be filled with stress, strife and confusion or the love, joy and peace of God?

Over 300 years ago a simple monk named Brother Lawrence learned some powerful secrets about living in God's presence. He discovered how to be filled with an amazing sense of love, peace and joy in the midst of demanding pressure from his job, physical pain, condemning thoughts and a multitude of voices (from within and without) clamoring for his attention.

In the early 1970's, when I was a very young Christian, someone placed in my hand a simple little book called 'The Practice of the Presence of God'. At first, it was very difficult for me to read because of the Old English vocabulary. But I persevered to the end, with dictionary in hand, and will be forever grateful I did.

More than ever, people need to learn how to walk with a sense of tranquil God's presence in the middle of challenging situations. The story of Brother Lawrence helped lay a foundation in my life that has enabled me to successful endure every situation I have faced over these past decades. His lifestyle and approach to God created a fresh perspective in me. I learned that I too could be filled with the loving Presence of God at all times and in all circumstances - whether they be positive or negative.

Realizing the great need for people everywhere to understand the wonderful truths shared by Brother Lawrence and the difficulty of this generation to understand Old English, I decided to make the reading of his conversations and letters much easier. It's with great joy I present to you this New Revised Version in Modern English of The Practice of the Presence of God. In this version I have also included a wider outside margins that enables the reader to make small notes and comments in the book as they discover Brother Lawrence's profound insights.

My prayer is that, through this book, you will learn how you can personally experience and be filled with the loving Presence of our gracious God at all times and in every circumstance!

Ephesians 3:19 - ...*to know the love of Christ which passes knowledge; that you may be filled with all the fullness of God.*

Jim Johnson, Missionary
July 2009
Berlin, Germany

Brother Lawrence
(Nicholas Herman)

★

In Herimenil, Lorraine, of France, Brother Lawrence was born Nicholas Herman sometime in early 1600's. The exact year of his birth is not clear since his birth records were destroyed in a fire, but it is estimated to be somewhere between 1605-1611. He was a young soldier and served in the Thirty Years War where he sustained a near fatal injury to his sciatic nerve. The injury left him crippled and in chronic pain for the rest of his life.

He was educated both at home and by his parish priest whose first name was Lawrence and who was greatly admired by the young Nicholas. He was well read and, from an early age, drawn to a spiritual life of faith and love for God.

In the years between the abrupt end of his duties as a soldier and his entry into monastic life, he spent a period of time in the wilderness living like one of the early desert fathers. In his characteristic, self-deprecating way, he mentions that he was a "footman (horse carriage valet) who was clumsy and broke everything".

At mid-life he entered a newly established monastery in Paris where he became the cook for the community that grew to over one hundred members. After fifteen years, his duties shifted to the sandal repair shop but, even then, he often returned to the busy kitchen to help out.

Brother Lawrence discovered and then followed, a pure uncomplicated way to walk continually in God's presence. For more than forty years, he lived and walked with an amazing sense of God at his side. Even so, through his own words, we learn that Brother Lawrence's first ten years were full of severe trials and challenges. A gentle man of joyful spirit, Brother Lawrence shunned attention and the limelight, knowing that outside distractions "spoils everything".

It was not until after his death that a few of his letters were collected. Joseph de Beaufort, counsel to the Paris archbishop, first published the letters in a small pamphlet. The following year, in a second publication that he titled, 'The Practice of the Presence of God', de Beaufort included four conversations he had with Brother Lawrence. In this small book of letters and conversations, Brother Lawrence simply and beautifully explains how to continually walk with God - not from scholarly knowledge but from the heart.

Unknowingly, Brother Lawrence passed on his secrets of living life in God's Presence. Those amazing insights are now gifts available to anyone who seeks to know God's peace and presence. Anyone, regardless of age or circumstance, can learn to practice his direct approach into God's Presence anywhere and at anytime.

Brother Lawrence's quietly died in 1691 soon after writing the last letter recorded in this book. His death was much like his monastic life where each day and each hour was a new beginning and a fresh commitment to love God with all his heart.

This was adapted from information provided by Lighthouse:
www.practiceGodsPresence.com
Used with Permission

First Conversation

★

Bro. Lawrence speaks with Joseph de Beaufort about his conversion and his work at the Monastery. He also shares his thoughts on faith, surrender and satisfaction in God's presence.

The first time I saw Brother Lawrence was on the 3rd of August 1666. He told me that God had done him a special favor - his conversion at the age of eighteen. Here are the things he shared with me:

That in the winter, seeing a tree stripped of its leaves, and considering that within a little time, the leaves would be renewed, and after that the flowers and fruit appear, he received a revelation of the Providence and Power of God, which has never since been erased from his soul. That this view had completely set him free from the world, and kindled in him such a love for God, that he could not tell whether it had increased during the forty years that he had since lived.

That he had been servant to the treasurer, and that

he was a very clumsy person who broke everything.

That he had desired to be received into the monastery, thinking that he would there be made to suffer for his clumsiness and the faults he committed, and that he should sacrifice to God his life, with its pleasures: but that God had disappointed him, since he had experienced nothing but satisfaction in that place.

That we should commit to experiencing God's Presence, by continually conversing with Him. That it was a shameful thing to quit conversing with Him to think of trivial matters and foolish things.

That we should feed and nourish our souls with high thoughts of God; which would yield great joy through our devotion to Him.

That we should enliven our faith. That it was lamentable we had so little faith; and that instead of taking faith for the rule of their conduct, men amused themselves with trivial devotions, which changed daily. That the way of Faith was the spirit of the Church, and that it was sufficient to bring us to a high degree of perfection.

That we should give ourselves to God, with regard both to natural and spiritual things, and seek our satisfaction only in the fulfilling of His will, whether He lead us by suffering or by consolation, for all would be equal to a soul truly yielded to God. That there needed to be faithfulness during the dry, unfeeling and frustrating times in which God tests our love for Him; that then was the time for us to make good and effective acts of consecration, simply one such act would often bring the spiritual growth needed.

That as for the miseries and sins he heard of daily in the world, he was so far from wondering about them, that, on the contrary, he was surprised there were not more, considering the malice sinners were capable of: that for his part, he prayed for them; but knowing that God, if He desired, He could remedy the mischief they did, so he didn't worry any more about it.

To arrive at the place of surrender as God requires, we should watch attentively over all the passions which mingle within us, in spiritual things as well as natural: that God would give light concerning those passions to those who truly desire to serve Him. That if this was my desire; sincerely to serve God, I could visit him (Bro. Lawrence) as often as I pleased, without any fear

of being trouble to him; but if not, that I should
not visit him again.

Second Conversation

★

Bro. Lawrence shares with Joseph de Beaufort on a variety of topics including the need for love to be the motive driving everything we do.

Brother Lawrence shared with me:

That he had always been governed by love, without selfish views; and that having resolved to make the love of God the end of all his actions, he had found reasons to be extremely satisfied with his method. That he was pleased when he could pick up a straw from the ground solely for the love of God, seeking Him only, and nothing else, not even His gifts.

That he had worried a long time about a belief that he would be damned; so strong was that belief that all the men in the world could not have persuaded him otherwise; but that he had come a resolution: I did not commit myself to a religious life except for the love of God, and I have endeavored to act only for Him; whatever becomes of me, whether I be lost or saved, I will always continue to act

purely for the love of God. I shall have this good
at least, that until death I shall have done all that is
in me to love Him. This worry of damnation had
lasted four years; during which time he had
suffered a great deal.

That since that time he had lived his life in perfect
liberty and continual joy. That he presented his
sins to God, telling Him that he did not deserve
His favors, but that God still continued to give
favor in abundance.

That in order to form a habit of conversing with
God continually, and referring all we do to Him;
we must first diligently approach Him: but that
after a little effort we will find without any
difficulty, His love inwardly exciting to us.

That he expected after the pleasant days God had
given him, that he should have his turn of pain and
suffering; but that he was not worried about it,
knowing very well, that as he could do nothing of
himself, God would not fail to give him the
strength to bear them.

That when an occasion of practicing some virtue
presented itself, he addressed God, saying, Lord, I
cannot do this unless You enable me; and that
then he received more than sufficient strength.

That when he had failed in his duty, he only confessed his fault, saying to God, I shall never change, if You leave me to myself; It is You who must prevent my falling, and change my faults. Then he didn't worry about it any more.

That we should approach God with great simplicity, speaking to Him frankly and plainly, and requesting His assistance in our life circumstances, the moment they happen. That it was his experience that God never failed to grant help.

That he had recently been sent to Burgundy, to buy wine for the monastery, which was a very unwelcome task for him, because he had no desire for business and because he was crippled, and could not get into a boat unless by rolling himself over the barrels. That in spite of that, he didn't worry about the journey or about purchasing the wine. That he said to God, it was His business he was doing, and that afterwards he found it very well performed. That he had been sent into Auvergne the previous year for the same reason; that he could not tell how he had done, but that it turned out very well.

So, likewise, in his work in the kitchen (to which

he had naturally a great aversion), having accustomed himself to do everything there for the love of God, and with prayer, upon all occasions, for His grace to do his work well, he had found everything easy, during the fifteen years that he had served there.

That he was very well pleased with the position he was now in; but that he was ready to quit, since he was always pleasing himself in every condition, by doing little things for the love of God.

That with him the set times of prayer were no different from other times: that he went off to pray, according to the directions of his Superior, but that he did not want that nor ask for it, because even his greatest work did not divert him from God.

That since he knew his obligation to love God in all things, and as he endeavored so to do, he had no need of a director to advise him, but that he needed much more a confessor to forgive him. That he was very sensitive to his faults, but not discouraged by them; that he confessed them to God but did not beg Him to forgive them. After he confessed, he peaceably resumed his usual practice of love and adoration.

That in his troubled mind, he had consulted nobody, but knowing only by the light of faith that God was present, he contented himself with directing all his actions to Him, i.e., doing them with a desire to please Him, no matter the outcome.

That useless thoughts spoil everything: that where mischief begins; but that we should reject them, as soon as we perceived their irrelevance to the matter in hand, or our salvation; and return to our fellowship with God.

That at the beginning he had often passed his appointed time of prayer, in rejecting wandering thoughts, and then falling back into them. That he could never regulate his devotion by certain methods like some people do. That nevertheless, after meditating for a short time, his mind would then wonder off in a manner that he could not explain.

That all bodily self-denial and other exercises are useless except as they serve to help us arrive at a union with God by love; that he had well considered this, and found it the shortest way to go straight to Him by a continual exercise of love, and doing all things for His sake.

That we should realize the great difference between acts of the understanding and acts of the will; that the first were comparatively of little value, and the latter is everything.

That our only job is to love and delight ourselves in God.

That all types of self-denial, if they are void of the love of God, could not erase a single sin. That we ought, without anxiety, expect the pardon of our sins through the Blood of Jesus Christ and only endeavor to love Him with all our hearts. That God seemed to have granted the greatest favors to the greatest sinners, as a sign of His mercy.

That the greatest pains or pleasures, of this world, were not to be compared with what he had experienced in a spiritual state: so that he worried about nothing and feared nothing, desiring only one thing of God; that he might not offend Him.

That he had no concern; for, said he, when I fail in my duty, I readily acknowledge it, saying, I am used to doing so: I shall never do otherwise, if I am left to myself. If I don't fail, then I give God thanks, acknowledging that it comes from Him.

Third Conversation

★

Bro. Lawrence discusses with Joseph de Beaufort his thoughts about: faith working by love; that natural work is no hindrance to sensing God's presence; and the need for complete surrender.

Brother Lawrence told me:

That the foundation of the spiritual life in him was the result of a high esteem of God in faith; which after he had well conceived it, he had no other cares, but faithfully to reject every other thought, that he might perform all his actions for the love of God. That when sometimes he had not thought of God for a while, he did not condemn himself about it; but after having acknowledged his wretchedness to God, he returned to Him with a much greater trust in Him, and therefore he found himself even more wretched to have forgot Him.

That the trust we put in God honors Him greatly, and draws us into great blessings.

That it was impossible, not only that God should

deceive, but also that God would let a person who is perfectly committed to Him suffer very long, and he resolved to endure everything for His sake.

That he had very often experienced the quick aid of Divine Grace on all occasions, that from the same experience, when he had work to do, he did not think of it beforehand; but when it was time to do it, he found in God, as in a clear mirror, all that was ready for him to do. That recently he had acted, without anticipating care; but before the experience above mentioned, he had used it in his affairs.

When outward work diverted him a little from the thought of God, a fresh memory coming from God filled his soul, and so inflamed and transported him that it was difficult for him to contain himself.

That he was more united with God during his natural work, than when he left his work for assigned times of prayer.

That he expected some great pain of body or mind; that the worst that could happen to him was, to lose the sense of God, which he had enjoyed for so long; but that the goodness of God assured him He would not completely forsake him, and that He would give him strength to bear whatever test He permitted to happen to him; and therefore that he feared nothing, and had no reason to consult with anybody about his situation. That when he had attempted to do so, he had always come away more perplexed; and that as he was conscious of his readiness to lay down his life for the love of God, he had no apprehension of danger. That perfect yielding to God was a sure way to heaven, a way in which we always have sufficient light for our conduct.

That in the beginning of the spiritual life, we should be faithful in doing their duty and denying themselves; but after that unspeakable pleasures followed: that in difficulties we only need to have access to Jesus Christ, and request His grace, with which everything becomes easy.

That many do not grow in their Christian faith, because they are stuck trying to earn God's forgiveness through penance, and particular exercises, while they neglect the love of God, which is the end. That this was revealed plainly by their works, and was the reason why we see so little solid godly character.

That people needed neither art nor science for going to God, but only a heart resolutely determined to apply itself to nothing but Him, or for His sake, and to love Him only.

Fourth Conversation

★

Brother Lawrence discussed with Joseph de Beaufort with great openness of heart concerning his approach to God.

He told me, that it all consists of one hearty renunciation of everything which we feel does not lead to God; that we should make a habit of continual conversation with Him, with freedom and in simplicity. That we only need to recognize God intimately present with us, to address ourselves to Him every moment, that we may press for His assistance for knowing His will in things doubtful, and for rightly performing those things which we plainly see He requires of us, offering them to Him before we do them, and giving Him thanks when we have done them.

That in this conversation with God, we are also devoted to praising, adoring, and loving him ceaselessly, because of His infinite goodness and perfection.

That, without being discouraged on account of our sins, we should pray for His grace with a perfect confidence, as relying on the infinite merits of our Lord. That God never failed offering us His grace for each action; that he distinctly perceived it, and never failed, unless when his thoughts had wandered from a sense of God's Presence, or he had forgotten to ask His assistance.

That God always gave us light in our doubts, when we had no other goal but to please Him.

That our spiritual transformation and character change did not depend on changing our works, rather doing for God, that which we commonly do for ourselves. That it was sad to see how many people mistook the means for the end, addicting themselves to certain works, which they performed very imperfectly, by reason of their human or selfish intentions.

That the most excellent method he had found for going to God, was that of doing our everyday work without any thought of pleasing men, [Gal. 1:10; Eph. 6:5-6.] rather (as far as we are capable) purely for the love of God.

That it was a great delusion to think that the times of prayer ought to be different from other times. That we are as strictly obliged to be joined to God during work and activity, as well as during prayer times.

That his prayer was nothing more than a sense of the presence of God, his soul being at that time unaware of anything but Divine love: and that when the appointed times of prayer were past, he found no difference, because he still continued with God, praising and blessing Him with all his might, so that he passed his life in continual joy; yet hoping that God would give him something to suffer, so he could grow stronger.

That we should, once and for all, heartily put our whole trust in God, and totally surrender ourselves to Him, secure that He would not deceive us.

That we should not get weary from doing little things for the love of God, who doesn't judge by the greatness of the work, but the love with which it is performed. That we should not get discouraged in the beginning, if we often failed in our endeavors, but we will eventually gain a habit, which will naturally produce its fruit in us, without our care, and to our exceeding great delight.

That the whole substance of religion was faith, hope, and charity; by the practice of which we become united to the will of God: that everything else doesn't matter and to be used as a means, that we may arrive at our end, and be swallowed up in it, by faith and charity.

That all things are possible to him who believes, that things are less difficult to him who hopes, things are more easy to him who loves, and still more easy to him who perseveres in the practice of these three virtues.

That the end we ought to propose to ourselves is to become, in this life, the most perfect worshippers of God we can possibly be, as we hope to be through all eternity.

That when we become spiritual we should consider, and deeply examine, what we are. And when we find ourselves worthy of all contempt, and those who do not deserve the name of Christians, subject to all kinds of misery, and numberless failures, which trouble us, and cause perpetual fluctuation in our health, in our frame of mind, in our internal and external dispositions: persons whom God would humble by many difficulties, inwardly as well as outwardly. After this, we should not wonder that troubles, temptations, oppositions and contradictions, happen to us from men. We ought, on the contrary, to submit ourselves to them, and bear them as long as God pleases, as things highly advantageous to us.

That the greater perfection a soul aspires after, the more dependent it is upon Divine grace.

Being questioned by one of his own monastery (to whom he was obliged to open himself), by what means he had attained such a habitual sense of God? He told him that, since his first coming to the monastery, he had considered God as the end of all his thoughts and desires, as the goal he should pursue to the end.

That in the beginning, when he was a novice, he spent the hours appointed for personal prayer in thinking of God, so as to convince his mind of, and to impress deeply upon his heart, Divine existence, instead of by devotion, and submission to the lights of faith, studied reasoning and elaborate meditations. That by this short and sure method, he exercised himself in the knowledge and love of God, resolving to use his utmost endeavor to live in a continual sense of His Presence, and, if possible, to never forget Him.

That when he had through prayer filled his mind with a great awareness of that infinite Being, he went to his appointed work in the kitchen (for he was cook for the monastery); there having first considered severally the things his job required, and when and how each thing was to be done, he spent all the intervals of his time, as well as before and after his work, in prayer.

That, when he began his work, he said to God, with a kinship trust in Him, "O my God, since You are with me, and I must now, in obedience to Your commands, apply my mind to these outward things, I ask You to grant me the grace to continue in Your presence; and to this end You will prosper me with Your assistance, receive all my works, and possess all my affections."

As he proceeded in his work, he continued a familiar conversation with his Maker, imploring His grace, and offering to Him all his actions.

When he had finished, he examined how he had discharged his duty; if he completed it well, he returned thanks to God; if otherwise, he asked forgiveness; and without being discouraged, he set his mind right again, and continued his exercise of practicing the presence of God, as if he had never deviated from it. "This way," said he, "by rising after my falls, and by frequently renewed acts of faith and love, I have come to a place, where it would be as difficult for me not to think of God, as it was at first to build the habit to think of

God."

Since Bro. Lawrence had found such value in walking in the presence of God, it was natural for him to strongly recommend it to others; but his living example was a stronger inducement than any arguments he could propose. His very countenance was edifying, such a sweet and calm devotion appearing in it, which could not but affect the beholders. And it was observed, that in the greatest hurry of his work in the kitchen, he still preserved his heavenly-mindedness. He was never hasty or lingering, but did each thing in its season, with an uninterrupted composure and tranquility of spirit. "The time of work," said he, "for me is not any different from the time of prayer; and in the noise and clutter of my kitchen, while several persons are at the same time calling for different things, I sense God in as great a tranquility as if I were upon my knees at the altar."

The Letters of
Brother Lawrence

First Letter

★

*Bro. Lawrence describes how the habitual sense of God's
Presence was found.*

Since you are so intent that I communicate to you
the method by which I arrived at this habitual
sense of God's Presence, which our Lord, in His
mercy, has been pleased to grant to me; I must tell
you, that it is with great difficulty that I am
pressured by your request; and now I do it only
upon the terms, that you show my letter to
nobody. If I knew that you would let it be seen, all
the desire that I have for your advancement would
not be enough for me to do it. The account I can
give you is:

Having found in many books different methods of
going to God, and different practices of the
spiritual life, I thought this would serve rather to
confuse me, than to facilitate what I sought after,

which was nothing but how to become wholly God's.

This made me resolve to give my all for the All: so after having given myself wholly to God, doing all I could about my sins, I renounced, for the love of Him, everything that was not Him; and I began to live as if there was none but Him and I in the world. Sometimes I considered myself before Him as a poor criminal at the feet of his judge; at other times I beheld Him in my heart as my Father, as my God: I worshipped Him as often as I could, keeping my mind in His holy presence, and recalling it as often as I found myself wandered from Him. This exercise was not easy, and yet I continued, notwithstanding all the difficulties that occurred, without condemning myself when my mind had wandered involuntarily. I made this my work all day long, as much as at the appointed times of prayer; for at all times, every hour, every minute, even into the height of my natural work, I drove away from my mind everything that was capable of interrupting my thought of God.

Such has been my common practice ever since I entered into Christian service; and though I have done it very imperfectly, yet I have found great value in it. These, I well know, are the result of the mere mercy and goodness of God, because we can do nothing without Him; and myself less than anyone else. But when we are faithful to keep ourselves in His holy Presence, and set Him always before us, this not only hinders our offending Him, and doing anything that may displease Him, at least willfully, but it also generates in us a holy freedom, and if I may say so, a familiarity with God, wherewith we ask, and that successfully, for the graces we stand in need of. To clarify, by often repeating these acts, they become habitual, and the presence of God becomes, as it were natural to us. Give Him thanks, if you please, with me, for His great goodness towards me, which I can never sufficiently extol, for the many favors He has done to so miserable a sinner as I am.

May all things praise Him. Amen.

Second Letter

★

Bro. Lawrence writes about the difference between himself and others. He consistently and persistently pursues faith alone. He disputes the charge of being delusional.

Not finding my way of life in books, although I have no problem with books, yet, for greater security, I shall be glad to know your thoughts concerning it.

In a conversation some days ago with a person of piety, he told me the spiritual life was a life of grace, which begins with slavish fear, which is increased by hope of eternal life, and which is consummated by pure love; that each of these conditions had its different stages, by which one arrives at last at that blessed consummation with the Lord.

I have not followed all these methods. On the contrary, I don't know why, I found that they discouraged me. This was the reason why, at my entrance into Christian service, I made a commitment to give myself up to God, to do the best I could about my sins; and, for the love of Him, to renounce everything besides Him.

For the first years, I commonly filled myself during the time set apart for prayer, with the thoughts of death, judgment, hell, heaven, and my sins. I continued some years applying my mind carefully the rest of the day, and even in the midst of my work, to the presence of God, whom I considered always with me and often in me.

After time I unconsciously did the same thing during my set time of prayer, which caused in me great delight and comfort. This practice produced in me such a high esteem for God, that faith alone was capable to satisfy me at that point. [I suppose Bro. Lawrence means that all distinct ideas he could form of God were unsatisfactory, because he perceived them to be unworthy of God, and therefore his mind was not to be satisfied but by the views of faith, which apprehends God as infinite and incomprehensible, as He is in Himself, and not as He can be conceived by human ideas.]

Such was my beginning; and yet I must tell you, that for the first ten years I suffered a lot: the worry that I was not devoted to God, as I wished to be, my past sins always present to my mind, and the great unmerited favors which God did for me, were the subject and source of my sufferings. During this time I fell often, and rose again soon after. It seemed to me that creation, reason, and God Himself were against me; and that faith alone was on my side. I was troubled sometimes with thoughts, that to believe I had received such favors was presumptuous, pretending to be where others difficulty arrive; at other times that it was a willful delusion, and that there was no salvation for me.

When I thought of nothing but to end my days of these troubles (which did not at all diminish the trust I had in God, and which served only to increase my faith), I found myself changed all at once; and my soul, which was constantly in turmoil, felt a profound inward peace, as if she were in her center and place of rest.

Ever since that time I walk with God simply, in faith, with humility and with love; and I apply myself diligently to do nothing and think nothing which may displease Him. I hope that when I have done what I can, He will do with me what He pleases.

As for what is now happening in me, I cannot express it. I have no pain or difficulty about my condition, because I have no will but that of God, which I endeavor to accomplish in all things, and to which I am committed, that I would not pick up a straw from the ground against His order, or from any other motive but purely that of love to Him.

I have discontinued all forms of devotion and set prayers but those to which my heart obliges me. And I make it my job to only persevere in His holy presence, where I keep myself by a simple attention, and a general fond regard to God, which I may call an actual presence of God; or, to better explain, an habitual, silent, and secret conversation of the soul with God, which often causes in me joys and raptures inwardly, and sometimes also outwardly, so great that I am forced to use means to moderate them, and prevent their appearance to others.

In short, I am assured beyond all doubt, that my soul has been with God more than ever during these past thirty years. I have skipped many things, that I may not be tedious to you, yet I think it is proper to inform you as to what I consider myself before God, whom I behold as my King.

I consider myself as the most wretched of men, full of sores and corruption, and who has committed all sorts of crimes against his King; touched with a deep regret I confess to Him all my wickedness, I ask His forgiveness, I abandon myself in His hands, that He may do what He pleases with me. This King, full of mercy and goodness, very far from punishing me, embraces me with love, makes me eat at His table, serves me with His own hands, gives me the key of His treasures; He converses and delights Himself with me ceaselessly, in thousands of ways, and treats me in all respects as His favorite. It is from this that I consider myself from time to time to be in His holy presence.

My most usual method is this simple attention, and such a general passionate regard to God; to whom I find myself often attached with greater sweetness and delight than that of an infant at the mother's breast: so that if I dare use the expression, I should choose to call this condition the bosom of God, for the inexpressible sweetness which I taste and experience there. If sometimes my thoughts wander from it by necessity or difficulty, I am quickly drawn back by inward feelings, so charming and delicious that I am ashamed to mention them.

I respectfully request you reflect rather on my great wretchedness, of which you are fully informed, than on the great favors that God does for me, as unworthy and ungrateful as I am.

As for my set hours of prayer, they are only a continuation of the same practice. Sometimes I consider myself a stone before a carver, where he can make a statue: presenting myself before God, I desire Him to make His perfect image in my soul, and make me entirely like Himself.

At other times, when I apply myself to prayer, I feel all my spirit and all my soul lift itself up without any care or effort of mine; and it continues as if it were suspended and firmly fixed in God, as in its center and place of rest.

I know that some charge that this condition is inactivity, delusion, and self-love: I confess that it is a holy inactivity, and would be a happy self-love, if the my soul in that condition were capable of it; because in effect, while it is in this tranquility, it cannot be disturbed by such acts as it was formerly accustomed to, and which were then its support, but would now rather hinder than assist it.

Yet I cannot bear that this should be called delusion; because the soul that enjoys God in this way, desires nothing from it but Him. If this is delusion in me, it is God's responsibility to remedy it. Let Him do what He pleases with me: I desire only Him, and to be wholly devoted to Him.

You will, however, oblige me in sending me your opinion, to which I always pay great attention, for I highly respect you, and am yours in our Lord.

Third Letter

★

Bro. Lawrence writes about a soldier friend whom he encourages to trust in God.

We have a God who is infinitely gracious, and knows all our needs. He will come in His own time, and when you least expect it. Hope in Him more than ever: thank Him with me for the favors He does you, particularly for the endurance and patience which He gives you in your afflictions: it is a plain mark of the care He takes of you; comfort yourself then with Him, and give thanks for all.

I admire also the fortitude and bravery of Mr. X. God has given him a good disposition, and a good will; but there is in him still a little of the world, and a great deal of youth. I hope the challenges which God has sent him will prove a wholesome remedy to him, and make him examine himself; it is an opportunity for him to put all his trust in Him, who accompanies him everywhere: let him think of Him as often as he can, especially during the greatest dangers. A little lifting up of the heart is satisfactory; a little remembrance of God, one act of inward worship, though upon a march, and sword in hand, are prayers which, however short, are nevertheless very acceptable to God; and far from lessening a soldier's courage in situations of danger, they serve to fortify it.

Let him then think of God the most he can; let him accustom himself, by degrees, to this small but holy exercise; nobody perceives it, and nothing is easier than to repeat often during the day these little internal adorations. Recommend to him, if you please, that he think of God the most he can, in the manner I am directing; it is very appropriate and most necessary for a soldier, who is daily exposed to dangers of life, and often of his salvation. I hope that God will assist him and all the family, to whom I present my service, being theirs and yours.

Fourth Letter

★

Bro. Lawrence writes of himself in the third person, and encourages his correspondent to press on to fuller practicing of the Presence of God.

I have taken this opportunity to communicate to you the sentiments of one of our members concerning the admirable effects and continual assistance he receives from the presence of God. Let you and me both profit by them.

You must know, his continual focus has been, for more than forty years that he has spent in Christian service, to be always with God; and to do nothing, say nothing, and think nothing which may displease Him; and this he has done without any other motive than purely for the love of Him, and because He deserves infinitely more.

He is now so accustomed to that Divine presence, that he receives from it continual help on all occasions. For about thirty years, his soul has been filled with joys so continual, and sometimes so great, that he is forced to use means to moderate them, and to hinder their appearing outwardly.

If there are times he is a little too much absent from that Divine presence, God makes Himself felt in his soul to recall him to Himself; which often happens when he is most involved in his natural responsibilities: he answers with prompt faithfulness to these inward drawings, either by an elevation of his heart towards God, or by a meek and fond regard to Him, or by such words as love forms on these occasions; as for instance, My God, here I am all devoted to You: Lord, make me according to Your heart. And then it seems to him that this God of love then satisfied with such few words, brings again tranquility and rests in the depth and center of his soul. The experience of these things gives him such an assurance that God is always in the depth or bottom of his soul, and renders him incapable of doubting it whatsoever.

Judge by this the content and satisfaction he enjoys, while he continually finds in himself such a great treasure: he is no longer in an anxious search after it, but it has opened before him, and he may take what he desires of it.

He complains much of our blindness; and cries often that we who satisfy ourselves with so little are to be pitied. God, he says, has infinite treasure to give, and yet we have a little emotional devotion, which passes in a moment. Blind as we are, we hinder God, and stop the flow of His graces. But when He finds a soul penetrated with a lively faith, He pours into it His graces and favors plentifully; there they flow like a torrent, which, after being forcibly stopped against its ordinary course, when it has found a passage, spreads like mad and in abundance.

Yes, we often stop this torrent, by the little value we set on it. But let's stop it no more: let's search ourselves and break down the bank that hinders it. Let's make way for grace; let's redeem the lost time, for perhaps we have little left; death closely follows, let's be well prepared for it; for we die but once, and a mistake there is irretrievable.

I say again, let's search ourselves. Time is pressing: there is no room for delay; our souls are at stake. I believe you have taken such effective measures, that you will not be surprised. I commend you for it, it is the one thing necessary: we must, nevertheless, always work at it, because not to advance, in the spiritual life, is to go backward. But those who have the gale of the Holy Spirit go forward even in sleep. If the vessel of our soul is still tossed with winds and storms, let's awake the

Lord, who assists in it, and He will quickly calm the sea.

I have taken the liberty to impart to you these good sentiments, that you may compare them against yours: they will serve again to kindle and inflame them, if by misfortune (which God forbid, for it would be indeed a great misfortune) they should be cooled. Let us then both recall our first fervor. Let's profit by the example and the sentiments of this brother, who is little known of the world, but known of God, and extremely caressed by Him. I will pray for you; do you pray instantly for me, who am yours in our Lord?

Fifth Letter

★

Bro. Lawrence prays for a sister who is about to make a commitment to Christian service. A fresh insisting upon the necessity and virtue of practicing the Presence of God.

Today I received two books and a letter from a sister, who is preparing to make her commitment to Christian service, and therefore desires the prayers of our members, and myself in particular. I perceive that she highly values them; please do not disappoint her. Beg of God that she may make her sacrifice in the view of His love alone, and with a firm resolution to be wholly devoted to Him.

I will send you one of these books that is about the presence of God; a subject which, in my opinion, contains the whole essence of spiritual life; and it seems to me that whoever faithfully practices it will soon become spiritual.

I know to practice it right, the heart must be empty of all other things; because God wants to the sole possessor of the heart; and since He cannot possess it alone, without emptying it of all else, so neither can He act there, and do in it what He pleases, unless it be left vacant for Him.

Not in the whole world is there a life more sweet and delightful, than that of a continual conversation with God: it can only be comprehended by those who practice and experience it; yet I do not advise you to do it with that motive; it is not pleasure which we seek in this exercise; but let us do it from a principle of love, and because God would have us do it.

Were I a preacher, I should above all other things preach the practice of the presence of God; and were I a director, I should advise the whole world to do it: so necessary I think it is, and so easy too.

Ah! If we only knew the need we have of the grace and assistance of God, we would never lose sight of Him, no, not for a moment. Believe me; make immediately a holy and firm resolution – to never more willfully forget Him, and to spend the rest of your days in His sacred presence, deprived of all consolation for the love of Him, if He thinks it necessary.

Set heartily about this work, and if you do it the way you should, be assured that you will soon experience the fruit of it. I will assist you with my prayers, poor as they are: I recommend myself sincerely to you, and those of your holy members.

Sixth Letter

★

Written to a member of the Monastery who had received from him a book, and to whom he again expounds on his favorite topic: encouragement to persevere.

I have received from a lady the things that you gave her for me. I wonder why you have not given me your thoughts about the little book I sent to you, and which you must have received. Pray fervently about the practice of it in your old age; it is better late than never.

I cannot imagine how religious people can live satisfied without the practice of the presence of God. For my part I keep myself separated to Him in the depths of the center of my soul as much as I can; and while I am so with Him I fear nothing; but the least turning from Him is insupportable.

This exercise doesn't fatigue the body much: it is, however, proper to deprive it sometimes, not often, of many little pleasures which are innocent and lawful: for God will not permit that a soul which desires to be devoted entirely to Him should take other pleasures than with Him; which is more than reasonable.

I do not say that because of that we must put any violent constraint on ourselves. No, we must serve God in a holy freedom, we must do our work faithfully, without turmoil or unrest; refocusing our mind on God gently and with tranquility, as often as we find it wandering from Him.

It is, however, necessary to put our whole trust in God, laying aside all other cares, and even some particular forms of devotion, though very good in themselves, yet those that are often unreasonably: because devotions are only a means to attain the end; so when by this exercise of the presence of God we are with Him who is our end, it is then useless to return to the means; but we may continue with Him our exchange of love, persevering in His holy presence: through acts of praise, of adoration, or of desire; through acts of yielding, or thanksgiving; and through all kinds of ways that our spirit can invent.

Don't be discouraged by the hostility which you may find in it from nature; you must not condemn yourself. At first, one often thinks it's a waste of time; but you must go on, and resolve to persevere in it to death, even with all the difficulties that may occur. I request the prayers of your holy members, and yours in particular. I am yours in our Lord.

Seventh Letter

★

At the age of nearly eighty, Bro. Lawrence writes to a man who is sixty-four, to live and die with God and promises and asks for prayer. [It is reported, during the 1600's only 5% of monks survived past 45 years of age.]

I pity you. It will be of great importance if you can leave the care of your affairs, and spend the remainder of your life only worshiping God. He requires no great matters of us; a little remembrance of Him from time to time, a little adoration: sometimes to pray for His grace, sometimes to offer Him your sufferings, and sometimes to return Him thanks for the favors He has given you, and still gives you, in the middle of your troubles, and to console yourself with Him as often as you can. Lift up your heart to Him, sometimes even at your meals, and when you are with others: the simplest little remembrance will always be acceptable to Him. You don't need to cry very loud; He is nearer to us than we are aware of.

To be with God, it is not necessary to always be at church; we may make our devotion from our heart, where we retreat from time to time, to converse with Him in meekness, humility, and love. Every one is capable of such familiar conversation with God, some more, some less: He knows what we can do. Let us begin then; perhaps He expects only one generous resolution from us. Have courage. We only have a little time to live; you are nearly sixty-four, and I am almost eighty. Let's live and die with God: sufferings will be sweet and pleasant to us, while we are with Him: and the greatest pleasures without Him, will be a cruel punishment to us. May He be blessed for ever. Amen.

Use your energies to worship Him, to seek His grace, to offer Him your heart from time to time, in the middle of your work, even every moment if you can. Don't always meticulously confine yourself to certain rules, or particular forms of devotion; but act with a general confidence in God, with love and humility. You can be assured of my poor prayers, and that I am their servant, and yours particularly.

Eighth Letter

★

Bro. Lawrence writes about wandering thoughts that occur during times of prayer.

You are not the only one who is troubled by wandering thoughts, this is nothing new. Our mind is extremely roving; but as the will is mistress of all our memories, it must recall them, and carry them to God.

When the mind, for lack of being sufficiently reduced by recollection, at our first engaging in devotion, has established bad habits of wandering and distraction, they are difficult to overcome, and commonly draw us, even against our wills, to the things of the earth.

I believe one remedy for this is, to confess our faults, and to humble ourselves before God. I do not advise you to use multiplicity of words in prayer; many words and long prayers often trigger wandering: hold yourself in prayer before God, like a dumb or paralytic beggar at a rich man's gate:

let it be your job to keep your mind in the presence of the Lord. If it sometimes wanders, and withdraws itself from Him, don't get upset with yourself; trouble and anxiety serve rather to distract the mind, than to refocus it; the will must bring it back in tranquility; if you persevere in this manner, God will have pity on you.

One way to refocus the mind easily during times of prayer, and to preserve it more in tranquility, is not to let it wander too far off at other times: you should keep it strictly in the presence of God; and being accustomed to think of Him often, you will find it easy to keep your mind calm during the times of prayer, or at least to refocus it from its wanderings.

I have told you already, in my former letters, of the advantages we may experience from practicing the presence of God: let's pursue it seriously and pray for one another.

Ninth Letter

★

Enclosing a letter to a corresponding sister, whom he regards with respect tinged with fear. He shares again concisely his reoccurring theme.

The enclosed is an answer to that which I received from a sister; please deliver it to her. She seems to me full of good will, but she wants to go faster than grace. A person does not become holy all at once. I recommend her to you: we should help one another by our advice, and yet more by our good examples. Please update me about her from time to time, and whether she is very fervent and obedient.

Let's remind ourselves often that our only work in this life is to please God, that perhaps everything besides this is folly and vanity. You and I have lived more than forty years in monastic life. Have we used our lives to love and serve God, who by His mercy has called us to this place and for that very end? I am filled with shame and confusion, when I reflect on the one hand, upon the great favors God has done, and constantly continues to do for me; and on the other, on the ill use I have made of them, and my small advancement in the way of perfection.

Since by His mercy He still gives us a little time, let us sincerely begin, let's redeem the lost time, let's return with a full assurance to that Father of mercies, who is always ready to receive us affectionately. Let's renounce - generously renounce, for the love of Him - all that is not Him; He deserves infinitely more. Let's think of Him perpetually. Let's put all our trust in Him: I don't have any doubt that we will soon see the fruit of it by receiving the abundance of His grace, with which we can do all things, and without which we can do nothing but sin.

We cannot escape the dangers that abound in life, without the actual and continual help of God; let's then pray to Him for it continually. How can we pray to Him without being with Him? How can we be with Him without thinking of Him often? And how can we often think of Him, accept by forming a holy habit of it?

You may tell me that I am always saying the same thing: it is true, for this is the best and easiest method I know; and as I use no other, I advise the world to use it too. We must know, before we can love. In order to know God, we must often think of Him; and when we come to love Him, we shall then also think of Him often, for our heart will be with our treasure. This is a truth that well deserves your consideration.

Tenth Letter

★

Bro. Lawrence has difficulty, but sacrifices his will, to write as requested to a person who has lost a friend and shares that his loss may lead to an acquaintance with the Friend.

I have had a good deal of difficulty to bring myself to write to you about your friend's loss, and I do it now purely because you desire me to. Please write the directions and send it to him. I am very pleased with the trust which you have in God: I wish that He may increase it in you more and more: we cannot have too much in so good and faithful a Friend, who will never fail us in this world nor in the next.

If your friend takes advantage of the loss he has had, and puts all his confidence in God, He will soon give him another friend, more powerful and more inclined to serve him. God does what He pleases.

Perhaps your friend was too much attached to the friend who died. We should love our friends, but without encroaching on the love of God, which must be the principal thing.

Please remember what I have recommended to you, which is, to think often on God, by day, by night, on your job, and even in your diversions. He is always near you and with you; don't leave Him alone. It would be rude to leave a friend who came to visit you alone: why then do we neglect God? Don't forget Him, rather think about Him often, adore Him continually, live and die with Him; this is the glorious job of a Christian; in a word, this is our profession, if we do not know it we must learn it. I will endeavor to help you through my prayers, and I am yours in our Lord.

Eleventh Letter

Bro. Lawrence is writing to someone who is in great pain and tells him God is the Physician of body and of soul and that he would gladly suffer at God's wish.

I do not pray that you may be delivered from your pains; but I sincerely pray that God would give you strength and patience to bear them as long as He desires. Comfort yourself with the One holds you fastened to the cross: He will set you free you when He thinks it is best. Those who suffer with Him are happy: accustom yourself to suffer in that manner, and seek from Him the strength to endure as much, and as long, as He judges necessary for you. The men of the world do not comprehend these truths, nor is it to be wondered at, since they suffer for what they are, and not as Christians: they consider sickness a pain to nature, and not as a favor from God; and seeing it only in that light, they find nothing in it but grief and distress. But those who consider sickness as coming from the hand of God, as the effects of His mercy, and the means which He uses for their salvation, commonly find in it great sweetness and emotional consolation.

I wish you could convince yourself that God is often (in some sense) nearer to us and more effectively present with us, in times of sickness than times of health. Don't rely on another Physician, for, I am worried that He reserves your cure for Himself. Then put all your trust in Him, and you will soon find the effects of it in your recovery, which we often hinder, by putting greater confidence in physics than in God.

Whatever remedies you make use of, they will succeed only if He permits. When pains come from God, only He can cure them. He often sends diseases of the body, to cure those of the soul. Comfort yourself in the sovereign Physician of both soul and body.

I foresee that you will tell me that I am very much at my ease, that I eat and drink at the table of the Lord. You have reason: but do you think that it would be easy for the greatest criminal in the world, to eat at the king's table, and be served by him, and for such favors to be enjoyed, without assurance of pardon? I believe he would feel extremely uneasy, and nothing could change that, except his trust in the goodness of God's sovereignty. So I assure you, that whatever pleasures I taste at the table of my King, yet my sins, ever present before my eyes, as well as the uncertainty of my pardon, torment me, though in truth that torment itself is pleasing.

Be satisfied with the condition in which God places you: however happy you may think I am, I envy you. Pains and suffering would be a paradise to me, while I should suffer with my God; and the greatest pleasure would be hell to me, if I could relish them without Him; all my consolation would be to suffer something for His sake.

I must, in a short time, go to God. What comforts me in this life is, that I now see Him by faith; and I see Him in such a manner as might make me say sometimes, I believe no more, but I see. I understand what faith teaches us, and, in that assurance and that practice of faith, I will live and die with Him.

Continue then always with God: it is the only support and comfort for your affliction. I shall call on Him to be with you. I present my service.

Twelfth Letter

★

Probably written to the same person. He expresses his own lasting comfort through faith.

If we were well accustomed to practice the presence of God, all bodily diseases would be greatly alleviated by it. God often permits that we suffer a little, to purify our souls, and oblige us to continue with Him.

Take courage, offer Him your pains unceasingly, pray to Him for strength to endure them. Above all, develop a habit of entertaining yourself often with God, and forget Him the least you can. Adore Him in your infirmities, offer yourself to Him from time to time; and, in the height of your sufferings, call on Him humbly and affectionately (as a child his father) to make you conformable to His holy will. I shall endeavor to assist you with my poor prayers.

God has many ways of drawing us to Himself. He sometimes hides Himself from us: but faith alone, which will not fail us in time of need, should be our support, and the foundation of our confidence, which must be completely in God.

I don't know how God will end my life: I am always happy: all the world suffers; and I, who deserve the severest discipline, feel joys so continual, and so great, that I can hardly contain them.

I would willingly ask God for a part of your sufferings, but realizing my weakness, which is so great, that if He left me one moment to myself, I would be the most wretched man alive. And yet I don't know how He can leave me alone, because faith gives me as strong a conviction as possible, that He never forsakes us, until we have first forsaken Him. Let's fear leaving Him. Let's always be with Him. Let's live and die in His presence. Do you pray for me, as I for you?

Thirteenth Letter

★

To the same person he exhorts him to have a fuller and complete confidence in God, for his body and soul.

I am in pain to see you suffer so long; what gives me some ease, and sweetens the feeling I have about your grief, is that they are proofs of God's love towards you: see them from that perspective, and you will bear them more easily. As for your situation, it is my opinion that you should discontinue human remedies, and resign yourself entirely to the providence of God; perhaps He is only waiting for that resignation and perfect trust in Him, to cure you. Despite all your care, physicians have up to now proven unsuccessful, and your malady still increases, it will not be tempting God to abandon yourself into His hands, and expect all from Him.

I told you, in my last correspondence, that He sometimes permits bodily diseases to cure the distempers of the soul. Have courage then: make a virtue of your needs: don't ask God for deliverance from your pains, but strength to bear resolutely, for the love of Him, all that He desires, and as long as He shall pleases.

Such prayers, indeed, are hard to pray, but most acceptable to God, and sweet to those who love Him. Love sweetens pain; and when one loves God, one suffers for His sake with joy and courage. I implore you to do so; comfort yourself with Him, who is the only Physician of all our problems. He is the Father of the afflicted, always ready to help us. He loves us infinitely more than we imagine: love Him then, and don't seek consolation elsewhere: I hope you will receive consolation soon. Goodbye. I will help you with my prayers, poor as they are, and shall be, always, yours in our Lord.

Fourteenth Letter

★

Bro. Lawrence expresses gratitude for the mercies and the amount of relief the recipient of this letter has experienced, while he has himself been near death, nevertheless he too has been comforted during his suffering.

I give thanks to our Lord, for having relieved you a little, according to your desire. I have been often near death, though I was never so much satisfied as then. Accordingly, I did not pray for any relief, but I prayed for strength to suffer with courage, humility, and love. Ah, how sweet it is to suffer with God! however great the sufferings may be, receive them with love. "It is paradise to suffer and be with Him; so that if in this life we would enjoy the peace of paradise, we must accustom ourselves to a familiar, humble, affectionate lifestyle with Him: we must prevent our spirits from wandering from Him: we must make our heart a spiritual temple by adoring Him unceasingly: we must watch continually over ourselves, that we don't do, or say, or think anything that may displease Him. When our minds are thinking about God, suffering will become full of unction and consolation.

I know to arrive at this place, the beginning is very difficult; for we must act purely in faith. But though it is difficult, we know also that we can do all things with the grace of God, which He never refuses to them who ask for it sincerely. Knock, persevere in knocking, and He will open to you in His due time, and grant you all at once what He has withheld for so many years. Goodbye. Pray to Him for me, as I pray to Him for you. I hope to see Him quickly.

Fifteenth Letter

★

Brother Lawrence wrote this letter soon before his death.

God knows best what we need, and all that He does is for our good. If we knew how much He loves us, we would always be ready to receive equally and with indifference from His hand the sweet and the bitter; everything is pleasing that comes from Him. The worst afflictions never appear intolerable, except when we see them from the wrong perspective. When we see them in the hand of God, who dispenses them: when we know that it is our loving Father, who humbles and pressures us: our suffering will lose its bitterness, and even become a form of consolation. Let all our effort center on knowing God: the more one knows Him, the more one desires to know Him. And as knowledge is commonly the measure of love, the deeper and more extensive our knowledge is, the greater will be our love: and if our love of God was great we would love Him equally in pains and pleasures.

Let's not amuse ourselves to seek or to love God for any natural favors that He has or may do in us. Such favors, though never so great, cannot bring us so near to God as faith does in one simple act. Let's seek Him often by faith: He is within us; don't seek Him elsewhere. Aren't we rude and deserve blame, if we leave Him alone, to busy ourselves about trivial things, which do not please Him and perhaps even offend Him? I'm afraid these trivial things will one day cost us dearly.

Let's begin to be devoted to Him with deep conviction. Let's cast everything else out of our hearts; He would possess them alone. Beg for this favor from Him. If we do what we can on our end, we will soon see that change that we aspire after working in us. I cannot thank Him sufficiently for the relaxation He has granted you. I hope from His mercy the favor to see Him within a few days. Let us pray for one another.

[Two days later he became bedridden and then died within the week.]

About the Author and his Wife

Jim and Priscilla Johnson were raised in the San Francisco Bay area of California and now live in Berlin, Germany. They have two grown children, James III and Christina along with three grandchildren.

Since their marriage in 1973 the Johnsons have served in virtually every function of church service and ministry, ranging from toilet cleaning to church planting. Even prior to their marriage - foreign missions was a deep passion in their hearts, beginning in 1972 with a missions trip to Mexico. Jim's travels have since taken him to 35 nations.

From 1991 through 1998 the Johnson family lived in Bulgaria, Eastern Europe where they founded and operated two Bible Schools, taught in other Bible Colleges, trained Christian leaders, hosted local and national conferences, served local churches and ministered throughout the nations of South Eastern Europe.

In Aug. 1998 they moved to Berlin, Germany where they initially served in two German churches. Responding to an intense burden to reach young adults in Berlin - in 2004 the Johnsons planted a new church they named RESET Berlin. Amazed at the progress of the church, they have hopes of planting more churches throughout the city.

Jim has a Bachelor of Theology degree from Pacific Coast Bible College in Sacramento, CA. Their home church is GateWay City Church, San Jose, CA.

July 2009 – Berlin, Germany

JimJohnsonMissions.com

Building Believers   Raising Leaders
Expanding the Kingdom of God

Missionaries

Jim and Priscilla Johnson

*We invite you to join us as we Impact the World
with the Love and Grace of our Lord Jesus Christ*

www.JimJohnsonMissions.com

Our Church in Berlin

*See the church and meet some of the
RESET Berlin members*

Free DVD Download
www.JimJohnsonMissions.com

Let's be Friends

Jim Johnson
jimjohnson@web.de

Books and Media by Jim Johnson

Transforming Grace – Paperback   Retail Price: $10.95

Practice the Presence of God – New
Revised Version in Modern English
Paperback   Retail Price: $ 7.95

Transforming Grace - eBook   Retail Price: $ 6.00
Journey with Jesus - eBook   Retail Price: $ 6.00
Powerfully Effective Prayer - eBook   Retail Price: $ 6.00
Practice the Presence of God - eBook   Retail Price: $ 6.00

Berlin Ministry DVD   Free Download

COMING SOON! More books are on the way so contact Jim directly for an up-to-date list!

Direct Orders:

> **20% Volume Discount** (For orders of 10 or more)
> Shipping & Handling costs will be added to the purchase price of all direct orders

For direct order purchases:
Email: jimjohnson@web.de
Or Visit: www.JimJohnsonMissions.com

Some Books by Jim Johnson may be purchased from:
  ➢ **Amazon.com**
  ➢ **CreateSpace.com**
  ➢

For more information contact Jim at: jimjohnson@web.de

Made in the USA
Middletown, DE
14 July 2023

35060646R00056